ASPERGER SYNDROME

P

616·858 832 YOU

By Ronnie Young

Cartoons:
Phil Hailstone

Published by:

Teachers' Pocketbooks
Laurel House, Station Approach,
Alresford, Hampshire SO24 9JH, UK
Tel: +44 (0)1962 735573
Fax: +44 (0)1962 733637
E-mail: sales@teacherspocketbooks.co.uk
Website: www.teacherspocketbooks.co.uk

*Teachers' Pocketbooks is an imprint of
Management Pocketbooks Ltd.*

With thanks to Brin Best for his help in
launching the series.

This edition published 2009.
Reprinted 2010, 2011.

ISBN 978 1 903776 99 5
E-book ISBN 978 1 908284 85 3

British Library Cataloguing-in-Publication
Data – A catalogue record for this book is
available from the British Library.

Design, typesetting and graphics by **efex Ltd**.
Printed in UK.

Contents

Foreword

When my son was first diagnosed with Asperger syndrome, at the age of 18, he was actually relieved. In fact, the first thing he said was, *'So there's nothing wrong with ME then; it's the Asperger that's causing the problems'*. Suddenly there was a reason for feeling always out of step; for knowing he was different from other children, and for the difficulties he had always had with misunderstanding his native language and getting into trouble for doing so.

The diagnosis also made me feel very guilty as a teacher, because looking back I recognised so many other undiagnosed children in my classes: Philip who could write wonderful philosophical argument but could not follow what I thought were 'simple' instructions; Jason, who would flap his hands whenever he was criticised, bringing huge peals of laughter from the other students; Carol, who was always in trouble as every piece of work she did, no matter the given subject, related to animals.

Foreword

Asperger syndrome can be a frightening diagnosis; it is a condition surrounded by myths and horror stories. I have written this book to shoot down some of those myths and to try to eradicate horror stories in the future. By explaining the syndrome and showing how to work successfully with students affected by the condition, I hope to dispel the dread many teachers experience when they see the words 'Asperger syndrome' on a child's statement.

A further aim is to help school staff identify the condition more easily. Most people with Asperger syndrome are undiagnosed; they are just thought of as 'odd' or 'weird'. At school they may have been suspended or excluded because of strange or difficult behaviour. This book will help teachers, LSAs and TAs to work *with* their students instead of against them, and to make sure the school is complying with disability law.

Foreword

I hope that indirectly, through teachers and support staff, the *Asperger Syndrome Pocketbook* will also help the parents of Asperger students, including those who may be in denial, or who have the condition themselves. Let those parents read this book and see that Asperger syndrome need not be a stigma – it is a difference in perception and understanding that can actually be a gift for many people.

Finally, and most importantly, this book is for the Philips, Jasons and Carols of this world so they can reach their full potential and be comfortable with who they are. I've lost count of the times I have heard a teacher say with amazement, *'There is more to this child than meets the eye'*. Yes, these children are 'different' – just as we all are. I hope this book helps you to rejoice in the differences and appreciate the quirkiness and originality of thought that Asperger students will bring to your class and school.

Once you tune in to the world of your Asperger students, the challenges outlined in the following pages will seem far easier to overcome. Working alongside your students on *these* challenges will help them with the much greater ones they face in a world that does not understand or tolerate difference.

What is Asperger Syndrome?

 Social Interaction

 Obsessive Interests

 Repetition & Change

 Verbal & Non-verbal Communication

 Whirling Mind & Unusual Sensitivities

 Anger & Rage

 Inclusion

What is Asperger Syndrome?

Welcome to Planet Asperger

It has been said that people with Asperger syndrome are aliens – in the nicest possible way. Indeed, Claire Sainsbury writing about school recollections from people with the condition called her book *'The Martian in the Playground'*.

Planet Asperger is a lonely little planet; it has just one inhabitant. It is located in a parallel universe which seems the same as the universe everyone else inhabits, but is actually very different. You see, Planet Asperger is governed by rules and laws which its sole inhabitant has figured out from the way he or she sees the world working. People with Asperger syndrome seem to lack intuition so work everything out by logic. This is fine until something goes against the established system, and in the real world – especially at school – this happens all the time. People *do* act out of character, classes *do* get moved to other rooms, teachers *are* substituted, seats *are* switched, and modules *do* come to an end.

Whenever a change happens, Planet Asperger starts to wobble. The student tries desperately to stabilise things and seek continuity. If stability and continuity are absent, panic ensues. This is when problems occur.

Welcome to Planet Asperger

What is Asperger syndrome?

Asperger syndrome is part of the autistic spectrum. This covers a number of conditions, including classic autism.

The syndrome is named after Hans Asperger (1906-1980), a Viennese psychiatrist who wrote a paper in 1944 (though not translated into English until the 1970s) based on his work with a group of boys who all showed similar characteristics:

- Failure to communicate effectively
- Poor social interaction
- Apparent lack of empathy
- Poor social imagination (working out other people's thoughts)
- Intense absorption in a special interest
- Problems with 'change'

How long has it been around?

Co-incidentally, Leo Kanner wrote *his* paper on autism in 1943 in New York, and it was initially accepted that two psychiatrists in two different places had 'discovered' the same condition at the same time.

However, in 1981, Lorna Wing, a British psychiatrist working with young autistic people, realised that not all people with autism were exactly the same. She identified a sub-group of youngsters whose characteristics were milder and who were able to function at a much higher level. It was she who presented the evidence that Kanner's syndrome and Asperger syndrome, along with other similar conditions, could be seen as component parts of an autistic spectrum.

It was not until 1991 that Asperger syndrome was recognised by the World Health Organisation and it was 1993 before the diagnostic criteria were written. So although Asperger syndrome has, in all likelihood, been with us for as long as human beings have existed, it is officially a very new condition.

What else is known about it?

Asperger syndrome is a developmental condition for which there is no 'cure', although there are many interventions that lessen its effects. Research into possible causes is ongoing – it is thought that genetic and environmental factors both play a part, but as yet nobody really knows why Asperger syndrome occurs.

People with Asperger syndrome, unlike those with autism, experience no significant language delay. Their IQ is at least average and, in many cases, extremely high. There are no accurate statistics on the prevalence of Asperger syndrome – many people have it so mildly they are just classed as being a bit 'odd' or 'eccentric'. This includes members of the older generation who have managed to function sufficiently to live reasonably normal lives. The National Autistic Society in 2008 gave a *probable* prevalence rate of about 1 child in 100. The ratio of boys to girls diagnosed with Asperger syndrome is about 4:1.

How do I recognise it?

So, what are the characteristics of Asperger syndrome? How do you recognise it? You will find the clinical diagnostic criteria at **www.aspergers.com/aspcrit.htm** but, generally, pupils with the syndrome will display *some* of the characteristics listed in *each* of the following five areas:

1. **Social communication**, eg:
- Not understanding facial expressions, gestures or tone of voice
- Not knowing when to start or finish a sentence, or which topics to talk about
- Shunning simple words, preferring complex or archaic language instead
- Difficulty with non-literal language such as metaphor, sarcasm, irony or street-talk

2. **Social interaction**, eg:
- Difficulty in making and maintaining friendships
- Problems understanding social rules or mores
- Becoming distressed with inconsistency and unpredictability
- Inappropriate behaviour such as tactlessness or apparent insults
- Apparent lack of interest in others

How do I recognise it?

3. **Social imagination**, eg:
* Inability to predict outcomes to situations
* Trouble understanding or interpreting others' thoughts, feelings or actions
* Having a limited range of interests which may be pursued rigidly or repetitively

4. **Sensory difficulties**, eg:
* Intensified or under-reaction to heat, cold or pain
* A need for constant noise or complete silence
* A need for very bright or very dim lighting
* Problems with touch, textures or colours

5. **Love of routines and fear of change**
Some pupils will show pronounced differences from the rest of your class; others will have such mild characteristics, you may not initially suspect Asperger syndrome. Remember, though, that for many people with very mild Asperger syndrome, the difficulties are just as great as for those with a more severe form: although they may *seem* the same as people without it, their thinking pattern is very different.

Is it a disability?

Asperger syndrome is not:

- A **physical** disability. Although the cause is physiological (believed to be a difference in the wiring of the brain) and it is a lifelong condition, it does not affect any part of the body adversely. There is no drug or medical intervention that can make it better

- A **psychological** disability. In some local authorities Asperger syndrome comes under mental health services, but it is not a psychiatric illness or psychological disorder. However, many people with the syndrome also suffer from anxiety and depression

- A **behavioural** disability. Many people with the syndrome also have ADHD or Tourette's syndrome but, in itself, it is not a behavioural condition. Inappropriate behaviour is usually because the planet is wobbling and the student is stressed

- A **learning** disability, although dyslexia and/or dyspraxia are very common in people with the condition and aspects of the syndrome can impede learning if not properly accommodated

Asperger syndrome and the law

Asperger syndrome *does* come under **disability discrimination law** because it is a recognised condition that lasts longer than 12 months and adversely affects the everyday functioning of the student to some degree. This means:

- Some pupils with Asperger syndrome may have a statement of special educational needs – but many with the condition do not. It is the latter who are often in trouble for inappropriate behaviour and who create the greatest challenges in and out of the classroom

- As teachers, you need to be aware of the signs so that appropriate strategies can be put into place for those without a statement

- Under the most recent legislation, the school has a duty to cater for all students' individual needs whether or not they are statemented and/or diagnosed

Plus points

So does Asperger syndrome always mean problems? NO! There are many plus points. Here's why it can be great to have Asperger students in the class:

Often, pupils with Asperger syndrome have a great memory. They will remember everything they are told, provided it is relevant, clear, unambiguous and logical

They are usually punctual, focused, reliable, dedicated and obedient. However, they have to be 'manually programmed'; they won't pick anything up by intuition

They are precise and pay great attention to detail

They do not understand guile, so what you see is what you get. You can expect loyalty and honesty. (Even when you would have preferred a white lie!)

They are independent thinkers

They are quirky, singular and eccentric, often with a marvellous sense of humour and refreshing outlook on life. They'll teach you as much as you teach them

Summary

- Asperger syndrome is part of a broader autistic spectrum. Those who have it vary in their degree of difference from those who don't have it
- There are fixed criteria which all have to be present to some extent for a diagnosis
- It does not come under any criteria for disability although it still comes under disability discrimination law
- There are many positive points about the syndrome

Some people find it easier to think of Asperger syndrome as a culture rather than a disability. It consists of differences, rather than deficiencies, and many people with the syndrome are happy with the **differences**. However, when we work with pupils from other cultures, we can dip into their culture and they can dip into ours. With Asperger pupils, *we* have to go to *their* world because *they* cannot come into *ours*. The following sections take you into the Asperger world, outlining the challenges and offering solutions.

What is
Asperger
Syndrome?

 Social
Interaction

 Obsessive
Interests

 Repetition
& Change

 Verbal &
Non-verbal
Communication

 Whirling Mind
& Unusual
Sensitivities

 Anger &
Rage

 Inclusion

Social Interaction

People interactions

Of all the challenges people with Asperger syndrome have to face, **social interaction** is probably the greatest. Of all the challenges teachers have to face with an Asperger pupil in the class, this is the area that causes the most problems.

People with Asperger syndrome see other people as machines. Every machine works differently from every other machine and none has a manual.

To complicate matters, each machine tends to operate differently from the way it worked a few minutes ago and how it will work in a few minutes time. This is why it is so important for you to **be consistent** when working with your Asperger pupils. Only when they have figured out how you operate can they actually work with you.

Inappropriate behaviour

The fact that the rules governing the behaviour of one machine do not necessarily apply to all the others is often what lies behind an Asperger pupil's **socially and emotionally inappropriate** behaviour.

If one teacher thinks it's fine for students to talk during activities, or is comfortable with them texting under the table, for example, it is bewildering – and sometimes distressing – for your Asperger pupil when other teachers have different (often unvoiced) expectations.

Furthermore, as you know, circumstances alter cases. Why is it OK to say things in a drama lesson or read out loud from a work of literature that you can't normally do or say in the classroom? Why is the rule never to run in a corridor when teachers do it in an emergency?

School is full of inconsistencies. The unwritten rules have to be explained to pupils with Asperger and contingencies put in place for when the rule does not apply.

Two unwritten codes of conduct

The lack of voiced expectations has all kinds of repercussions for pupils with Asperger syndrome because, in fact, there are **two** unwritten codes of social conduct in school. The first is the one the teachers know and assume their students know, ie the one about how to behave. It includes sharing, taking turns, lining up in the playground, not telling tales on your classmates and being polite.

Think back to your own school days. How did you know these things? My guess is that you just picked them up from the other children. Unfortunately, people with Asperger syndrome do not just 'pick things up'.

Example 1.
When the teacher went out of the classroom for a few minutes, she warned the class not to talk. When she came back she asked *'Did anyone talk?'* Sarah put her hand up and reeled off a list of the guilty parties.

The first unwritten code – two more examples

Example 2.
At the beginning of the swimming lesson, Andrew had got undressed before realising his mum had forgotten to pack his trunks. He panicked because he knew he would be in trouble and did not know what to do – so he rushed out to ask his teacher, completely oblivious to the fact that he was naked.

Example 3.
Zac's class was told to line up in the playground. He knew what a line was, but had no idea where he was supposed to stand in it – so he placed himself at the front of it after the line had formed.

Just as they see people as machines, pupils with Asperger operate as machines. Everything that you want them to do, you have to tell them explicitly – a form of manual programming, if you like. Input the rule, wind them up and off they go.

The second unwritten code

The second unwritten code is the one the pupils share. It may be to do with the latest street language; or the correct designer labels; or which are the coolest bands or cartoon characters; or even which football team to support.

What is certain is that whilst the other kids will have picked up what is OK and what isn't, no-one will have thought to tell your Asperger student, especially if the pupil has few friends in the first place. This means s/he will be even more isolated, maybe even a figure of fun, out of step with the others.

Cracking the code – strategy

Encourage discussion about what is 'in' and what is 'out'. PHSE lessons, circle time and tutor group sessions are ideal for this. Discuss with all your pupils the differences between popular, transient culture and traditions and explain why, for example, football supporters are partisan. This will stand them in good stead for their general curriculum – English, history or geography, for example, where it is good to be able to put forward a case and to look at differences.

Pupils with Asperger will have their own views, though. They may think the local football team is rubbish and this can cause some problems – so teach how to argue and discuss. The further up the school you go, the more this skill is necessary.

As a teacher, you may welcome the idea of a student who is skilled in argument and rhetoric, but a word of warning: your student with Apserger syndrome, being totally logical, will always win an argument. Battles of wills are always to be avoided.

Following 'the rules'

Once Asperger pupils learn and understand 'the rules', life should get easier.
After all, planet Asperger is governed by rules. As long as your pupils know what they should be doing at any given time, they will feel secure and confident.

Problems can arise, though, if Asperger pupils see other pupils breaking the rules and getting away with it. You can lessen Asperger stress (and improve behaviour generally) by checking your whole school behaviour management policy:

* Is what is OK and what is not OK clear and unambiguous?
* Are the sanctions for inappropriate behaviour clear?
* Are they applied consistently no matter who the student and who the teacher?

You need to be able to answer 'yes' to all of the above.

Friendship problems

The most common question I am asked by teachers is *'How can I get my Asperger student to make friends?'* The simplest answer is: *'You can't'*.

Young children with Asperger syndrome are usually quite happy playing on their own or going somewhere quiet to read or play on the computer. Some children are actually quite scared of going into a crowded and chaotic playground and do not want to run around with others. Children with Asperger syndrome tend to be self-sufficient. They like being loners, especially if they are boys.

This all seems to change at adolescence, though. Suddenly it seems that everyone else is having a marvellous time because of 'friends' – maybe a best buddy, maybe a gang, maybe even a girlfriend or boyfriend. There is also tremendous pressure to have a friend. Parents worry about an unpopular child; teachers feel uncomfortable about an isolate in the class and the other children see a 'Johnny-no-mates' as a prime target for bullying and teasing. Books, television and films and music all extol the excitement and fun you get from friendship.

Four stages of friendship

So your Asperger student decides to make a friend – but it all goes horribly wrong. The reason for this can be seen in the typical evolution of friendship skills.

In their book *'Young Friends'*, Roffey, Tarrant and Majors argue that friendship skills develop in four stages during childhood. At pre-school age, children change from playing *alongside* someone to playing *with* them, turn-taking, sharing and becoming less possessive of equipment.

Between the ages of 5 and 8 they understand an element of reciprocity and a need to maintain the friendship. During pre-adolescence their friendships are based on similarity, on shared intimacies and shared exploration. They offer each other emotional support and are increasingly aware of how they may be viewed by others.

By adolescence, the point at which most young people with Asperger enter the game, friendships are based on trust, higher levels of self-disclosure and mutual or admired aspects of personality.

Four stages of friendship

Without having developed the skills and experience of the earlier stages of friendship, Asperger pupils' teenaged attempts to make friends will be clumsy and stilted, lacking any understanding of what friendship is and what it means.

Add to this the regular horrors of adolescence: self-consciousness, burgeoning sexuality, mood swings and then complete the picture with the Asperger characteristics of naivety, misunderstandings, social ineptness and lack of awareness – and it is not surprising it all goes wrong.

As teachers we need to be aware of the particular vulnerability of students with Asperger syndrome at adolescence. Their naivety and trusting nature means they are easy prey for 'false friends'. They can be led into crime because somebody talked them into it and made false promises; they may be put into humiliating or dangerous situations as a dare or they may be placed in compromising situations sexually or with drugs. Social skills training (see page 32) can address these matters.

Friendship strategies

Friends do not have to be in the same age group or class. When we make friends as adults it's usually because of a shared interest or hobby. This principle works well for Asperger students in school. Find out what they enjoy, and introduce another student who supports the same football club, plays chess to a similar level, enjoys the same computer game, etc. It need not be someone in the same class or yeargroup as your student.

People with the syndrome are usually highly skilled at and have great knowledge of their interests. What a wonderful asset to have as a friend someone with this degree of knowledge or skill!

Always highlight your students' talents and skills rather than their deficiencies – especially to them. And it's also worth highlighting that at any age it's OK to be a loner – some people think it's a gift. You don't have to wait for someone to be free to go to town – you can go alone. There are lots of activities you can do on your own, especially to do with your special interest.

Social skills training

The majority of people take for granted their ability to:

- Behave appropriately in any given situation
- Understand non-verbal communication
- Have a conversation

People with Asperger syndrome find all of these problematic and need to be taught the necessary skills. Some schools use drama teachers or specially trained support staff to run social skills training sessions at lunchtimes with their Asperger students.

Sessions like these can be particularly supportive during adolescence, which is a tough time for all youngsters, but with no 'mates' to help you through, it's even harder. As for all students, things get better in time, but your Asperger teenager may not understand this, so your support and wisdom are essential.

However, the teaching of social skills is beneficial for *all* children, and all teachers can contribute to a programme that is delivered, for instance, in circle time, or in PSHE or tutorial time. If the whole class is involved it will reinforce classroom relationships by helping all students to understand differences in others.

Social skills training

Social skills sessions may include topics such as:
- Relationships with other children and staff
- How to open a conversation with someone new
- How to give compliments
- Understanding the difference between banter, teasing and bullying
- How to share and take turns
- Imagining or predicting different outcomes to given situations
- Interpreting body language, gestures and facial expressions
- Understanding tone of voice
- Offering and receiving criticism
- What is OK to say or do in public and what should be kept private

There are some excellent books to support social skills training. You will find a selection listed at the back of this book.

Group work

Working in groups is a fundamental part of school life. Pupils with Asperger syndrome will hate working in groups, and many will find it very difficult. These few strategies will help:

1. A group does not have to be more than three – and for the Asperger student the fewer people in the group the better.
2. Don't tell your class to 'get into groups' – this will be extremely difficult for any Asperger pupil. It is better if *you* organise the groups.
3. Where possible, give everyone in the group a task – for example: *John, read paragraph 1, Julie read paragraph 2 and Jasmine read paragraph 3. Then each of you tell the other two, in that order, what you read'.*
4. If it is a brainstorming session, give your student a specific role, such as scribe. The most frightening thing about group work for an Asperger student is the lack of structure – so you need to put it in.

Social imagination

The ability to understand and interpret other people's motivation, thoughts and feelings is always lacking to some degree in people with the syndrome. Your Asperger student may not see that certain comments they make can cause offence or embarrassment, nor that an apology can go some way to making others feel better.

This lack of social imagination makes it difficult to understand the concept of lying – so your student will be invariably honest. This, of course, brings other problems. If you rashly promise something and conveniently forget about it, an Asperger pupil will always remind you. If you decide to give someone the benefit of the doubt during a perceived behaviour issue, your Asperger student may feel aggrieved if the 'promised' sanction is not forthcoming.

Miss...when are you going to eat your hat?

Lies and diplomacy

The common dishonesties we use in social niceties – white lies or diplomatic withholding of comments, for example – are particularly difficult for people with Asperger syndrome. We bring up our children to be honest and in school honesty is promoted as essential for the wellbeing of all. So why are white lies acceptable, indeed preferred, in certain situations?

Why do we tell people we feel very well when we have a cold coming on?

Why do we say *'I don't need help'* when we obviously do?

Why do we talk about Father Christmas and the Tooth Fairy?

Why is it OK to say *'your dress matches your eyes'* and not *'your dress matches your gums'*?

Give simple rules

If we find white lies, euphemisms and diplomatic withholding of negative comments difficult to categorise and explain, these are almost impossible concepts for someone with Asperger syndrome to grasp.

Again, social skills training is the best way to help your student. Simple rules that are regularly reinforced can give a framework, eg:

> **Never make personal remarks unless asked**

PSHE and circle time are good forums for the whole class to discuss honesty, lying, diplomacy and euphemisms. You can talk about inference and underlying intentions in books read or programmes watched. Again, this is useful for all students, not just those with the syndrome.

Fixations on people

Sometimes, Asperger pupils will fixate on particular people – especially if that person has been nice to them in the past. They may interpret a throwaway remark incorrectly or misinterpret body language (see next section). Whatever the reason behind the fixation, your student may be accused of stalking, or worse, when this is not what they intended. Remember your student lacks intuitive understanding of the relevant social rules. You must talk to them about what is OK and what is not. Make some rules, eg:

> *'You can come to my room at break and I will talk to you then, but if I am not there you must wait. If I have not returned by the end of break you must go to your class.'*

> *'You must not follow Molly around as she does not like it. If you do you will get into trouble.'*

Make all rules clear, unambiguous and logical – and make sure you follow up with any threatened or promised consequences every time.

Summary

- Asperger students see people as machines, operating to a set of rules. Until they learn how you operate, they will not be able to work efficiently with you

- Asperger students will not know the unwritten social codes and mores understood by staff and/or students unless somebody informs them of their existence

- Rules are a comfort to Asperger students as long as they are clear, the sanctions for not obeying them are clear, and they are upheld consistently by all staff

- Lack of friends is often less of a problem to the Asperger student than to parents, teachers and other pupils. Instead, encourage 'mates' – students or staff with a shared interest

- Group work needs careful thought and forward planning by the teacher

- Social skills training is important for students with the syndrome

- Asperger students may not understand that others have thoughts and feelings different from their own. They are usually honest – often to their detriment

- Inappropriate fixations on people must be tackled clearly by making rules

What is Asperger Syndrome?

 Social Interaction

 Obsessive Interests

 Repetition & Change

 Verbal & Non-verbal Communication

 Whirling Mind & Unusual Sensitivities

 Anger & Rage

 Inclusion

Obsessive Interests

And what are you interested in?

Not all people with Asperger syndrome appear to have an obsessive interest, but the vast majority do. Dealing with this can be very challenging for some teachers:

'He won't stop drawing pictures of monsters – is he very disturbed?'

'Jennifer is always a problem in food technology because she will only cook or eat food that is yellow.'

'If I hear anything else about Dr Who I'll scream!'

'I've had to confiscate his books on birds because he will insist on reading them when I'm trying to teach him maths.'

More than a hobby

Lots of people without Asperger syndrome have a hobby that takes up much of their time. However, the obsessive interests of the vast majority of people with the syndrome are more than just hobbies. Tony Attwood describes them as *'solitary, idiosyncratic and (they) dominate the person's time and conversation'*. They differ from a compulsive disorder in that *'the person really enjoys their interest and does not try to resist it'*.

Nobody has a definitive explanation for this characteristic of Asperger syndrome. What is universally acknowledged, however, is its importance. Whatever your pupil's 'specialist subject', it has been chosen by them and they will have an encyclopaedic knowledge of it. Their interest fulfils certain roles and once you understand this, you can use it in a positive way.

Being in control

The interest is a place of safety. Whenever planet Asperger begins to wobble, this is the one secure place that does not change.

Dean Beadle, a young man with Asperger syndrome describes how *'in times of great stress, my obsession provides me with those rare moments of calm'**. Therefore, the worst thing you can do in school is to take it away, whether as punishment or in ignorance of its importance. Just as you may use a hobby or activity to de-stress, Asperger pupils take refuge in their 'specialist subjects'.

The difference is that whereas you may be able to de-stress by going running or having a glass of wine after school, when things get too much for pupils with Asperger syndrome, the de-stressor is needed urgently, as a coping strategy. In a changing and bewildering world with lots going on, it is the one thing they can control.

In this sense, the obsessive interest is a valuable way of alerting you to the fact that your Asperger pupil feels out of control and may need urgent support or time out. Keeping a record of these moments can also help you to identify what triggers their distress so you can adjust the environment accordingly.

*Communications Magazine, National Autistic Society, Summer 2008

Use the obsession positively

'Specialist subjects' can also be very useful for accessing the curriculum. James, a maths teacher, was struggling to engage Danielle because all she wanted to do was talk about the Napoleonic Wars, so he combined the two. When he taught area, he measured the battlefields; when he taught ratio it was illustrated by the number of weapons the French had compared with the British. The rest of the class loved it. In fact, they said it was the most interesting year of maths they had ever had.

Obsessive interests are also useful as motivational tools or rewards. If your pupil is refusing to do a piece of work, try this: *'If you do ten minutes of maths you can have five minutes drawing dinosaurs'*. Set clear and consistent boundaries around the obsessional behaviour.

Further positive uses

Another great way of using the obsession is to raise your pupil's self-esteem.
Tony was an expert on Manchester United. His teacher asked everyone in the class to think of really difficult questions to ask him. He could answer them all. This raised his standing in the class as well as making him feel good.

It is often difficult to work out what someone on the autistic spectrum is thinking, especially if they communicate little. Dean Beadle suggests looking at the obsession might throw light on this. He feels his own obsession with Dr Who is to do with his desire for freedom. It may also be linked to a subconscious wish to work with beings that do not have human feelings or inconsistencies.

And still more positive uses

The obsessive interest is certainly a way into communicating with your pupil. You can teach social skills through it or use it as an entry into a school club. Exploit it in drama or the arts to make your pupil feel included. Use it to explore literature or as a topic in French or Spanish; it will enrich your teaching as well as your pupils' learning.

Finally, it may be a route into the world of work. Matthew had an obsession with toilets. His learning support assistant always knew when he was stressed, as the cloakroom would be flooded. Any items left lying around Matthew had dropped down the loo. She invested in a shredder and whenever he earned a reward Matthew was allowed to put a handful of shredded tissue into the pan. Matthew became a sanitary engineer. He now designs bathrooms.

Summary

- Obsessive interests are very important to people with Asperger syndrome – if you remove their interest, you are taking away their place of security and comfort, and a major coping strategy
- Obsessive interests can be used in positive ways, eg to warn you of your pupil's state of mind, as a way of accessing the curriculum, and as a bargaining tool
- Your pupil's encyclopaedic knowledge can be used to raise self-esteem
- Use the obsession as a line of communication, to teach social skills or to work with others in a school club
- The obsession may hold the key to a future career

What is Asperger Syndrome?

 Social Interaction

 Obsessive Interests

 Repetition & Change

 Verbal & Non-verbal Communication

 Whirling Mind & Unusual Sensitivities

 Anger & Rage

 Inclusion

Repetition & Change

Old routines, new routines

At the beginning of the book we talked abut Planet Asperger and its inhabitant's need for sameness. There are plenty of repetitive routines in school that are calming and that fulfil the need for order and knowing what is coming next, eg lessons following the same format, break at the same time each day, always lining up in the same order, etc.

BUT think of all the changes that happen in school all the time – room, subject, teacher, curriculum, module, seat, neighbour, textbook…

For someone with Asperger syndrome, each September can be like starting a new school all over again, especially if class groupings have been changed, with, for the Asperger student, a new batch of machinery to learn to operate.

We can't avoid change in school – but with a little forward planning, we can pre-empt it. Among the most useful aids are timetables.

Timetable

This is a real timetable for a real teenager, but the format can be adapted for pupils of any age. James only felt secure if every minute of every day was planned.

MON		Mr Ja...	home... Blue file, pencil case, calculator, ruler, homework book	LUNCH	Mr... Yellow file, pencil case, ruler, calculator, textbook	GO HOME	& WATCH TV	Physics Assignment
		Blue file, pencil case, calculator, ruler, notebook						
TUE		**MATHS** Pure E2 Mr Gul Yel. File Ruler Calc. P.C.	**BIOLOGY Lab 9** Dr Brewer Red file, pencil case, lab coat, goggles, notebook	LUNCH	GO HOME	REVISE BIOLOGY	EAT & WATCH TV	GO TO THE GYM
WED	TUTORIAL D16 Notebook	**PHYSICS** L104 Mr James Blue file PC, Calc, nb HWK	**FREE** Library – revise biology Red file, pencil case, ruler, notebook	LUNCH	**BIOLOGY LAB 3** Dr Brewer Red file, pencil case, pencils, notebook ROOM CHANGE THIS WEEK ONLY	GO HOME	EAT & WATCH TV	Maths Assignment
THU	BIOLOGY E2 Dr Brewer Red file, PC, note book	**PHYSICS L101** Mr James Black file, pencil case, ...ulator...		LUNC	**I.T.** Learning Centre Mary Smith Green file, discs, textbook	GO HOME	EAT & WATCH TV	Revise Biology and STOP at 10

Forward planning

Mary, his form tutor, was happy to help as much as she could (though she refused to sort out his weekends and holidays). She drew up his basic timetable on the computer and asked all his teachers to tell her by Friday morning what James would need for the following week.

James and his tutor met every Friday lunchtime and went through the timetable together. The squares with the diagonal line mean 'This is your free time and you can do what you like – but if you want we can discuss it'. James needed to know when to go home (this was a 6th form college), when to eat and when he could watch TV. He needed to know when to start his homework and when to stop (see Thurs. evening). He needed to know in advance if there was a room change (see Weds). He also needed to check he had the correct equipment for his lessons.

James needed to refer to his timetable constantly in September, but by February he just needed the security of it being in his pocket. By the following September, he was able to construct his own timetable which included holiday periods and revision.

Further support

However, because this was real life, unforeseen changes sometimes occurred, so Mary also met James at 8.30 each morning and 1.30 each afternoon so they could amend his timetable if necessary. She also gave James her own timetable so if something untoward and totally unplanned happened, he had somewhere safe to go.

Classroom and lesson timetables also work well with younger children, especially if you use pictures and colour. Having them in clear view is useful in primary schools. Younger children may also need further help with what to do in times of panic, for example, through social stories.

Tip: Always have a back up member of staff whom your student can go to should you be absent. The fact that you are not where you should be is a change in routine.

Rigidity of thought

Many people with Asperger syndrome become research academics because they can spend their whole lives working on one tiny detail. Unfortunately, that skill is not so useful in the classroom where you might find your student does not want to stop what they are doing and move on.

So make a rule and stick to it. Tell your student *'You have only five more minutes to spend on this task'*. Use props to help with this, such as egg-timers, hour-glasses, alarm-clocks; anything that the student can see counting down will be useful. Maybe the teacher or learning support assistant can warn *'two minutes to go... one minute to go'*.

It is also helpful if an outline for the lesson or session can be displayed somewhere so the pupil knows where you are in the lesson and what will be coming next.

Remember – you are trying to avoid sudden change.

Fixations and rigidity

Teachers of Asperger children are sometimes confronted with a pupil asking the same question over and over again. This is common in people with the syndrome. It means Planet Asperger is wobbling; the pupil is looking for stability and 'sameness'.

- Don't vary the answer you give, not even by using slightly different vocabulary or altering the word order
- Don't lose your temper
- Don't refuse to answer

It can be wearing having to answer the same question 25 times in the same way, but there are a couple of useful strategies you can employ:

- Tell your student, *'I will answer this only five times because that is the rule,'* and do so, counting each answer
- If your pupil is literate, ask them to write down the question and then you write down the answer. The pupil can then look at it each time the planet wobbles

Summary

- Forward planning can pre-empt many of the problems posed by change
- Detailed timetables are very useful tools
- Meet your student at fixed points in the day to warn him/her of any unforeseen changes
- Warn the student in good time when activities in lessons are going to change
- Deal with repetitive questioning by providing the stability and sameness the pupil is seeking

What is Asperger Syndrome?

 Social Interaction

 Obsessive Interests

 Repetition & Change

 Verbal & Non-verbal Communication ◀

 Whirling Mind & Unusual Sensitivities

 Anger & Rage

 Inclusion

Verbal & Non-verbal Communication

What do you mean?

People with Asperger syndrome find communication very difficult. They take what is said literally and so their perception is that people rarely say what they mean or mean what they say. For example, when you said, 'Take your books out', did you mean out of your bag or out of the room?

Or when you spoke, did you speak ironically or metaphorically, or perhaps you implied (rather than stated explicitly) what you meant?
Not only that, the words we say account for only a fraction of how we communicate. We also use:

- Tone of voice
- Body language
- Facial expression
- Pauses
- Eye contact
- Silence

Unless you teach these methods of communication to pupils with the syndrome, they will be aware that there is a whole communication system out there that means nothing to them. This section looks first at verbal challenges then at non-verbal ones.

Literal and implicit meaning

George, a year 11 student, was on work experience. His boss asked, 'Do you know where the post office is?'

'Yes,' said George.

'Good,' said his boss, 'I need you to take this letter.'

So off George went. He was gone for five hours. His boss was frantic. When George finally returned, his boss demanded to know where he had been.

'I took the letter to X,' (which, fortunately, was only to the other side of town) said George.

'But I asked if you knew where the post office was, and you said you did,' said his boss.

'I do know,' said George, 'but you asked me to take the letter.'

This is a perfect example of how if *you* don't make the connection explicit, your Asperger student will not infer. Say what you mean!

Inferring meaning

The difficulty with interpreting implied, or otherwise subtly expressed, meaning can pose particular challenges for Asperger pupils in English comprehension and in studying literature, especially poetry. Unless, of course, you have put in place the correct support, such as clear teaching of imagery or a study guide to remind your student.

Josh had been well taught about imagery and only needed a few pointers with his poetry. When he studied a poem by Dylan Thomas, the first verse of which is:

> *'Do not go gentle into that good night*
> *Old age should burn and rave at close of day;*
> *Rage, rage against the dying of the light.'*

he found the analysis and appreciation easy, as soon as he realised how the metaphor of day/night corresponded to life/death.

Taking it literally

What will people who understand things literally make of the following?

- *'His voice has broken'*
- *'Let's toast the bride'*
- *'My mother's going to kill me when I get home'*
- *'Has the cat got your tongue?'*
- *'Come on, pull your socks up'*

The most serious incident I heard was of a
little boy who fell in the canal and made no
effort to save himself because the sign said
'no swimming'. Someone jumped in
to rescue him.

Some strategies for literality

Don't stop using metaphorical or idiomatic language with Asperger pupils, just be aware of when you do, and if your pupil looks bewildered or puzzled, explain the metaphor. Don't make it into a joke or assume the child is being deliberately difficult; just gently point out what you do mean. People with the syndrome do not want to do or say the wrong thing and are mortified if they inadvertently do.

The best approach is to teach the difference between literal and metaphorical language as early as possible. Teach it in English or literacy lessons and reinforce it in other subjects. It can be the stimulus for some fun lessons and makes a good basis for social skills training.

The head of year grilled Pete and Mike for 20 mins

Imagery

The Asperger student with a good grasp of imagery and linguistic device will come up with wonderful original metaphors of their own:

'The car was rocking with every movement and the road slithered jerkily forward. Although the windscreen wipers were flapping valiantly, they were fighting a losing battle as the rain drove harder.

Suddenly there was a large bang. The car skidded a few metres and the steering wheel took on a mind of its own. What could I do? I got out to investigate. One of my tyres had burst. My heart sank to the cellars of my body. The nearest civilization had been fifteen miles back. What was I going to do?

Out of the car, I could see my surroundings. Wild moorland was visible when lit up by the lightning with rows of trees scattered around it. There were tall, sharp and majestic trees, which reached high and stabbed the heavens. There were also bare, scrawny and rather eerie looking trees whose tortured souls cried out to me. The rain was still pelting down but a strange silence hung in the air.'

Jonathan Young, 1993
(Year 10 student with Asperger syndrome)

Implications for exams

Although our first instinct may be to laugh at the naivety of somebody who takes metaphors literally, it can actually be very frightening if we do not know what we can believe and what we cannot. Not only that, there are some serious implications. The following are all taken from public examination papers:

1. Can you label this diagram?

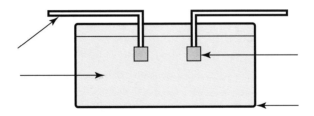

Likely Asperger response: 'Yes' (or 'No') before moving on to the next question.

Implications for exams

2. Julius Caesar landed in Britain in 55 B.C. How long ago was that?

Asperger answer: *A very long time ago.*

3. How would you prioritise these reasons for London being a major tourist centre?

a) Historical buildings
b) Famous theatres
c) High quality shopping areas
d) Eateries of all nationalities
e) Excellent transport links
f) Beautiful architecture

Asperger answers could include: *'in a list', 'one after the other', 'with difficulty'.*

Unfortunately, many examination questions are ambiguous.

Strategies for interpreting exam questions

The obvious strategy is to go over lots of practice exam questions so students get used to 'examiner speak' and are able to interpret instantly what a question means.

However, from 1st September 2007, an amendment to the Disability Discrimination Act 2005 means that public examination bodies are obliged to make 'reasonable adjustment' for anyone taking general qualifications – which includes SATs, GCSEs, A levels and vocational qualifications.

One reasonable adjustment that a school obtained for their Asperger student was a separate room for just that student and a member of staff known to him. The teacher was allowed to say *'What does this question mean?'* If the student correctly identified the meaning of the question, he went on to answer it. If not, the teacher said *'No, try again'* – and the student kept trying until he got the correct meaning. The member of staff was NOT allowed to tell the student what the question meant and was NOT allowed to give any help with the answer.

Strategies for interpreting exam questions

If a required adjustment is written into a diagnosis or statement, it will facilitate matters at the exam board, although under the Disability Discrimination Act 2005 the student does not actually have to have either a diagnosis or statement to qualify for 'reasonable adjustment'. Asperger pupils will almost certainly need extra time in exams because of having to make so many attempts at interpreting the question.

If you have difficulty obtaining the appropriate adjustments for your students, the Equality and Human Rights Commission (www.equalityhumanrights.com) will be able to advise you further.

(See page 117 for other practical ways to make exams more Asperger-friendly.)

Melody of speech

When listening to someone with Asperger syndrome, you may notice little variation in the pitch, tone, stress or rhythm of their speech. They are largely unaware of intonation, which means there is no point in *you* using it to communicate meaning.

Look at how the message in one sentence can change depending on where you place the emphasis:

- **I** didn't say she stole my money (but someone said it)
- I **didn't** say she stole my money (I said something else)
- I didn't **say** she stole my money (but I thought it)
- I didn't say **she** stole my money (but someone stole it)
- I didn't say she **stole** my money (but she did something with it)
- I didn't say she stole **my** money (but she stole someone's)
- I didn't say she stole my **money** (but she stole something else of mine)

There are seven different interpretations of this sentence according to where you place the stress. Which will your Asperger student understand?

*From **Making Friends: A Guide to Getting Along with People** by Andrew Matthews.*
Published by Media Masters, 1990

Strategies for teaching melody of speech

Music therapy has been found to be invaluable in teaching rhythm and emphasis. Amelia Oldfield has written several very useful books explaining how to use it in the classroom (see page 124). It is fun for all children, not just those with the syndrome.

You can also practise reading and play games with intonation to show how emphasis alters meaning, eg:

- For younger children, simple games such as slowly counting numbers and putting emphasis on random ones, at which point all the children must suddenly sit down or stand up or turn round are fun

- Cloze exercises (passages of text with missing words) are also a fun way to show how putting in, taking out and substituting certain words alters meaning

Pedantic language

Pedantic or over-formal language may become a feature of Asperger speech during childhood or adolescence. This may show itself in the use of unduly complicated language. For example, eight-year-old Lisa was not impressed by the vegetarian restaurant she was taken to and asked if, next time she had a meal out, she could go to 'an omnivore restaurant'.

Sometimes, extremely formal or textbook language may be used. Laurence, who was studying A level biology, used Latin names for all plants and animals – all correct and all accurately spelt. However, his teacher did not know all the Latin names and assumed Laurence was *'trying to be clever'*. When he marked Laurence's work with, *'Use the proper names for these'*, Laurence became very distressed. They *were* the correct names.

Ask yourself: does it matter? It may be that over-formal or complex language affects your pupil's ability to communicate with their peers, in which case it may be another subject for social skills training; otherwise, just appreciate your pupil's facility with language and accept it as an idiosyncrasy.

Neologisms and idiosyncratic language

People with Asperger syndrome have a wonderful facility to invent words or phrases and to use language in an original and creative way. It will all be entirely logical, and it gives an interesting insight into how an Asperger mind works.

Asperger students invented the following. Have a go at working out what they refer to. (Answers at foot of page.)

1. Egg poles.
2. Hopping sticks.
3. Tidying down.

Answers:
1. Egg cups on a stem, shaped like wine glasses.
2. Crutches.
3. When the mess is on the floor and you have to get down to tidy it.

The art of conversation

You may think conversation is straightforward: I speak, you listen, then you speak and I listen. In fact, conversation is more like this:

I speak, you listen, you interpret, you listen, you process, you listen, you decide what you're going to say, you listen, you rehearse, and maybe adapt what you're going to say, you listen, you wait for me to stop talking – you speak.

But how do you know when I have stopped talking?

- Obviously, I stop speaking – but maybe this is a pause for breath or a dramatic pause
- My tone of voice may go up or down – but people with the syndrome don't recognise this
- My body language or facial expression may change – but again, people with the syndrome may not recognise this

The art of conversation

Having a conversation is fraught with difficulties for people with Asperger syndrome.

Your pupil may suddenly interrupt you when you are speaking or may not reply when you want them to speak. They may have spent so long just interpreting what you have said that they haven't followed your line of reasoning, so they come in with something they rehearsed at the beginning of your speech – or they may be so worried about what to say that they say something completely irrelevant, maybe something to do with their obsessive interest.

Although most of us grow up with an inherent ability to converse, this is not the case for people with Asperger syndrome. They may need to be formally taught how to have a conversation, and especially how to recognise conversation cues.

Recognising conversation cues

- Try analysing passages of dialogue with your student. Discuss possible ways in which characters have known when to start speaking

- Look at soap operas on television and study how characters' voices or facial expressions change during conversations

Body language and facial expressions

Body language is a foreign language to people with Asperger syndrome. They will not just have 'picked it up', which is why some people with the syndrome use the wrong body language – or none at all. Similarly, they will not understand other people's use of it. Like a foreign language, it must be taught.

The same goes for facial expressions. They are meaningless to someone who has not learnt to interpret them. This can lead to all sorts of problems – not recognising signs of dissatisfaction or annoyance, for example, and becoming confused when criticised (or punished) for not complying with the hidden intentions or signals.

Equally, the Asperger student's own facial expressions may be inappropriate, eg showing total revulsion at another student's accidental injury, which can lead to the idea that the student has no feelings or empathy.

Body language and facial expressions

People with the syndrome DO have feelings but they don't usually know how to react to other people's feelings. They may recognise that someone is feeling sad, but because they themselves don't feel sad, they don't know what facial expression to use other than the one they naturally have at the time. This is why they may laugh when they see someone else who is very unhappy, or just ignore them, because they haven't themselves caused the other person's sadness.

The National Autistic Society has an excellent range of books and resources to help teach facial expressions and body language (see pages 123-5). This is such an important element of being able to function in society, it should be the linchpin of any social skills programme. It can be easily reinforced in the classroom using some of the ideas on the next page.

Teaching facial expressions and body language

- Study facial expressions in art
- Use drama to understand emotions more readily
- Talk about how a character in a story might be feeling and what his face may look like
- Use photographs from newspapers and magazines to talk about body language and facial expressions, and use a mirror so the student can see his/her own expressions

A fun way of working with this topic is to show old episodes of a soap opera like *EastEnders* with the sound turned off. Pause the recording and see if the student can work out what may have happened to the character.

Eye contact

Lack of eye contact is a major cause of frustration for teachers and LSAs working with people on the autistic spectrum. There are several reasons for its absence:

*   Unless someone has explained it, the pupil will not realise the importance of eye contact and how the eyes are regarded as being a measure of emotion. (The student may not understand the emotion, never mind be able to measure it!)

*   If you tell your pupil, *'Look at me when I am speaking to you'* and they look at your hand or your foot, they are doing what you told them to. If you require eye contact, you need to say, *'Look into my eyes when I am speaking to you'*

*   If you are in a foreign country where you can just about get by with the language, you don't look into someone's eyes when they are talking to you, you watch their mouth. Your speech, full of metaphors, incomplete sentences and pauses may seem like a foreign language to an Asperger student. If they have to look at you at the same time as trying to work out what you are saying, the mind will have stimulation overload

Eye contact

If you really want eye contact, you may have to teach it. It *may* come naturally, provided you are totally consistent, clear and unambiguous with everything you say. But don't be surprised if you are met with a constant, glassy-eyed stare.

But is it really that important?

When you feel there really *needs* to be eye contact – at an interview, for example, prepare the student adequately and warn the interviewer in advance that there may not be much eye contact. Above all, do not burden the student with more expectations and opportunities for failure. The more relaxed and in control the student feels, the more likely it will be that eye contact comes naturally.

Summary

- People with the syndrome take language literally and have real problems with imagery, metaphor, implied meaning and ambiguous language
- This can have serious implications for public examinations if students are not taught examiner speak
- Pitch, emphasis and intonation are not understood
- Some students with the syndrome may use pedantic or overly-formal language and often use language in an idiosyncratic or totally original way
- Conversation is difficult as people with Asperger syndrome do not understand communication cues
- Facial expressions and/or body language may be inappropriate, misinterpreted or absent
- Eye contact may need to be taught

What is Asperger Syndrome?

 Social Interaction

 Obsessive Interests

 Repetition & Change

 Verbal & Non-verbal Communication

 Whirling Mind & Unusual Sensitivities

 Anger & Rage

 Inclusion

Whirling Mind & Unusual Sensitivities

Ever decreasing circles

People with the syndrome find it very difficult to filter out unimportant details. Marc Segar, a young man with Asperger syndrome, described his thinking as *'ever decreasing circles which trapped every thought, idea and emotion I had ever had'*. The Asperger brain is a constantly moving whirl, rather like a kaleidoscope of colour and shapes.

Sometimes an idea or thought will work its way up to the surface, and your student may suddenly react, for instance by bursting into laughter. Maybe they just remembered a funny film they saw last week and have reacted to that. Similarly, an Asperger student who suddenly swears out loud or bangs their fist on the table may have remembered being bullied when younger and have been overwhelmed by anger.

It's important to understand that these inappropriate outbursts are just reactions – the student needs to be refocused on the task in hand.

Marc is now deceased, but his sister has given her permission for this quote.

Unconventional sleep patterns

A major implication of this inability to switch off the brain is the difficulty that many people with the syndrome have with sleep. It is not unknown for them to be awake for 24 or even 36 hours then suddenly exhaustion overtakes them and Zzzzzz… – they fall asleep – on the bus, in class, on the sports field, in their school dinner. They will sleep until they are refreshed and WOW! – up they get and the whirl starts again.

If your pupil falls asleep is there somewhere they can go, such as a medical room or an office? Remember, they are not sleepy because they have been up enjoying themselves the night before. More likely, they will have been wide awake in bed worrying because they are not sleeping.

Worry is very common in people with the syndrome. Their problems with rigidity of thought, coupled with difficulties in communicating feelings, exacerbate anxieties and threaten to overtake them.

What to do about worries

At school we inadvertently collude with this worry.

> On his first day in year 5, Michael was told,
>
> *'Remember that every lesson and every piece of work you do between now and May will be important for the SATs'.*
>
> The rest of Michael's class did not really begin to worry until April. Not so Michael. He was so anxious about May that he was unable to function properly from September onwards.

If you are working with someone with the syndrome, help them to put worries and anxieties into perspective. Encourage them to list worries as soon as they become an issue, and make time to discuss them. Help your student break down tasks into smaller chunks and show them how to make mini deadlines. Teach them to manage their time – possibly with the use of timetabling.

More strategies to clear the mind

Visual Mapping. Try to get as much as possible out of the head and on to paper. Ask your pupil to list everything that's worrying them. Excellent software is now available that allows brainstorming straight on to the computer (see page 125). The programme then organises it into a flowchart, linear diagram or mind map. This kind of visual mapping will help your student to clear their mind

Relaxation Techniques. A good way to switch the brain off momentarily. Some schools practise yoga or meditation with pupils at the beginning of the school day or at the start of certain lessons and have found it improves concentration and outcomes

Time Out. Always remember that worries lead to chronic anxiety, which leads to stress. Time out is a tried and tested way of moving a student to a place of sanctuary where they can switch off their brain and do something else. A dedicated time out room is ideal, but just allowing the student to leave the classroom with the LSA and to walk around for a few minutes is often enough to relieve their tension

Sensitivities

Many people with Asperger syndrome are over- or under-sensitive to sensory stimuli: For example:

- Oliver cannot work at all if he hears someone breathing
- Alisha gets very distressed by certain smells, especially cosmetics or toiletries
- Rhiannon will wear only soft clothes like sweatpants, and this breaks the school's uniform code
- Andrew cannot bear messy or gooey materials, eg mud or papier maché, near his skin
- Chris wraps his legs in tight tape as he is comforted by the feeling of restriction

Such sensitivities can cause huge problems in the classroom, triggering emotional outbursts or inappropriate behaviour. The next pages list the most common sensitivities with suggestions for overcoming potential problems.

Sight and smell

 Pupils may be over- or under-sensitive to sunlight or may prefer to play or sit in the dark

Can they wear sunglasses or a hat outside? Is there a dark area they can go to if things get too much for them? Can they move seats?

 Pupils may be sensitive to certain colours of light or rapid changes from light to dark or bright patterns or moving images

Don't flick lights on/off to get attention. Do you need coloured gels and overlays? Can you change the background colours of SMART board and computer screens? Can you change the colour of light bulbs?

 Many students are sensitive to strong or sweet smells, especially of cosmetics or toiletries, but maybe the smell of the school bus or the toilets

Ask staff to use unscented soap and to avoid wearing perfume/aftershave. Suggest the student sniffs a hankie sprayed with something that they like, or that they rub Vaseline round their nostrils to reduce the strength of smells

Hearing

 Students may be over-sensitive to sound (breathing, hum of the fluorescent light, others talking, the computer fan)

Ear plugs are one suggestion, or 'noise buster' headphones

 Some Asperger pupils may be very distressed by loud and sudden noise, such as the bell or the fire alarm. Conversely, they may be oblivious to noise and not realise they are humming or singing as they work

Countdown the bell with the student at 3, 2, 1 minute intervals so s/he is ready. If a fire drill is planned, try to warn the student in advance of the alarm. Humming or singing may satisfy a need for physical stimulation to the face or throat. Try a mini-massager to face and ear, or get them to stroke their face or throat

Taste

 Students may have a very limited diet or may seek out very spicy or sour foods, or only crunchy foods or foods of just one colour

 They may very strongly prefer hot or cold food, or refuse to eat any food mixed together, as in sandwiches

If these preferences cannot be accommodated in school lunches, what about a packed lunch? Respect your students' wishes – we all have food preferences!

Touch

This is often the sense that causes most difficulties and is least obvious to others.

Some textures may be horrible for Asperger students to touch. This includes furniture, the floor or carpet, their clothes, learning materials, or even themselves
Experiment with different textures. What DO they like to touch? Can you put a soft cushion on a hard chair? Can they wear soft tights under rough trousers? Does your pupil HAVE to work with clay or plasticine? Can you adapt or change the uniform policy? Can you cut tags out of clothes?

Pupils may need to touch or stroke things for comfort
Make a rule limiting this, 'You may do this five times'. Try a koosh ball (a ball made of rubber filaments attached to a soft core) *or bendy toy*

Sometimes they may want to lick inappropriate things. This will have hygiene implications
If there are some things they must NEVER do, make this into a rule, but substitute something they CAN lick

Touch

 Students may need to do things with their body – rock, spin or flap their hands. They need the sensation of rhythm or body awareness

Allow frequent movement breaks; let them go outside and move around. Younger children may love rhythmical songs or a drum to bang if the lesson allows. Older children may like pushing against a wall or having a short run

 Many pupils have issues with breezes and wind. They cannot sit in a draught (although you may not feel it) or feel the wind in their hair

Seat the student elsewhere, encourage wearing a hat outside

 Some students may hate to be touched; others may crave a hug or embrace

The latter may affect your school's 'touching' policy and the former may have implications for PE

The most difficult situations for many children are in the playground at break where there is so much stimulation all at once. You may have to make alternative arrangements.

Summary

- People with the syndrome find it difficult to filter out unwanted details and their heads are full of constantly whirling ideas, thoughts and emotions
- If sudden inappropriate behaviour occurs, it may be caused by a random thought coming to the surface
- Sleeping is often difficult and students may suddenly fall asleep at inappropriate times in school
- Try not to worry students too much in advance
- Help students to manage their worries and anxieties by discussing them regularly and find strategies for them to cope
- Try to get as much as possible out of the brain and on to paper
- Under-or over-sensitivity can cause stress and inappropriate behaviour, so be aware of triggers and ways to manage particular sensitivities

What is Asperger Syndrome?

 Social Interaction

 Obsessive Interests

 Repetition & Change

 Verbal & Non-verbal Communication

 Whirling Mind & Unusual Sensitivities

 Anger & Rage

 Inclusion

Anger & Rage

Meltdown!

As we have seen, school can be extremely stressful for students with Asperger syndrome and because they have difficulty communicating that stress, it may go unnoticed. It can build up so that a seemingly trivial incident may be the one that provokes a hugely disproportionate verbally or physically aggressive act. These tantrums or rage attacks – quick sudden and extreme – are sometimes described as a **neurological storm**, or **'meltdown'**. The student will be completely out of control, screaming, throwing furniture or even physically attacking someone else.

This does not happen with all students with the syndrome (and not all students who have rage attacks have Asperger syndrome!); however, it is one of the key concerns teachers have about working with students with the syndrome, hence its inclusion in this Pocketbook.

The rage cycle

There is a wealth of books and articles on the rage cycle (including the *Anger & Conflict Management Pocketbook* by Paul Blum). Mitchell Beck and Linda Albert, along with Brenda Smith Myles and Jack Southwick are particularly helpful in explaining the cycle and strategies to avert it. Their work has informed my own practice. I've recommended books from some of these authors on page 124.

Albert and Beck talk about a three-stage cycle:

It is helpful to look at each of these stages and to consider effective strategies to support students and pre-empt these distressing incidents.

The rumbling stage

Although rage attacks appear to come from nowhere, there are actually warning signs. If recognised early, rage can be avoided.

Think about the times *you* feel angry. What are the slight behavioural or physical changes that happen to you? They differ from person to person, but often include: faster heartbeat, sweaty palms, feeling hot, knotted muscles, tight in chest, etc.

This is **the rumbling stage** when full-blown rage *can* be averted. If you know your students, you may be able to spot the characteristics of impending anger, eg:

- Repetitive body movement, eg rocking a chair, feet or pencil tapping
- Biting lips or nails
- Complaining of feeling unwell (not realising the horrible feeling in their tummies is anger, not sickness)
- Swearing, raising voice or muttering under breath
- Fidgeting, screwing up paper or scribbling on a page

Strategies at the rumbling stage

If you intervene at the rumbling stage, you can often avert meltdown! Here are some ideas to try when you spot the early warning signs.

Run a message
Engineer an errand to get the student out of the room, eg to collect a folder from a distant part of the school (a folder that you have placed there for just such an emergency). This will allow the student time to calm down and to get rid of some nervous energy and adrenaline. By the time they return the problem has abated. Sometimes the rumbling student will realise what you are doing and be grateful you have saved him or her from the humiliation of raging in front of fellow students.

Tell me…
Walk over to your student and engage them in a conversation about their special interest area. This distraction technique works in a similar way to preventing a toddler having a tantrum.

Strategies at the rumbling stage

Get in touch
Sometimes a comforting hand on a shoulder or on a jiggling knee or tapping hand can be calming. However, this can be a high risk strategy. Check your school policy on 'touch' and know in advance whether your student is happy with this kind of physical contact.

Up close
As you walk around the room, move close to your student. People with the syndrome hate attention being called to themselves or their behaviour and for some students your calm presence will be enough for them to calm down as well.

Sign language
Work out some prearranged signals so your student can pick up your message from your body language, eg: if I scratch my nose and look at you it means *'I know you have a problem and I am coming to talk to you about it as soon as I have finished this instruction'*.

Strategies at the rumbling stage

Cartooning

Provided you teach the strategy to the student in advance, 'cartooning' is an excellent way to help them focus on something other than their growing anger.

Imagine it is the first lesson after lunch and Jenny comes in with a white face and clenched fists. You know something has happened and anger is brewing. You ask Jenny to draw what has happened.

This is what she draws:

Strategies at the rumbling stage

Cartooning

Cartooning has several advantages for Jenny:

- She has something physical to do with her hands. I have seen students break pencils and tear paper with the vehemence with which they draw. Better that than tear and break themselves or others

- The other students are getting on with their work, unaware of what Jenny is doing, so preserving her dignity and privacy

- It prevents the need for articulation, where Jenny would have got more emotional and possibly other students would have wanted to join in

- When the drawing is finished, Jenny can get on with her work and you have an objective record of what happened that you can discuss later

- You can ascertain a pattern of behaviour which triggers Jenny's distress and you can keep the cartoons to use as the basis of social skills training

Strategies at the rumbling stage

Time out
Have a named place of safety where students can go to gain control. Maybe they can take their work in with them or maybe it is a place where they can just be quiet.

Walking without talking
This strategy, explained in more detail by Smith Myles and Southwick (see page 124) is much easier for an LSA than a class teacher as it requires taking the student out of the room and walking around the school or grounds with them until they have calmed down. It's important not to talk, because that will put added pressure on the student (and it raises the possibility of saying the wrong thing!) When they are ready to talk, have a conversation and when they are ready to rejoin the class, accompany them.

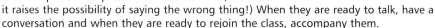

The rage stage

If one of your students does reach the meltdown stage, don't panic. Just have a drill in place and everyone will stay calm. Tried and tested procedures include:

- Isolating your student by getting the others out of the classroom
- Making sure another member of staff is notified (just in case help is needed)
- Making sure the room is as safe as possible by pushing back desks and chairs
- Speaking in a quiet, low, slow voice to your student using reassuring phrases such as *'it's OK, I'm here, don't worry'*. Your student will probably not be listening to the messages as they are so absorbed in getting rid of the angry feelings – but the sound will be comforting and mesmerising and will help to bring them down faster

The whole thing may seem like three hours, but will probably be more like three minutes.

The recovery stage

Your student will feel exhausted after the rage and may need to sleep. They will also feel embarrassed and horrified to have lost control in front of others. They are now at risk of a different kind of anger manifestation – hurting themselves in some way. For this reason, never leave a student on their own after a rage attack. They need firm, non-judgemental, supportive closure. So, once they have fully calmed down help them to understand their feelings and explore ways to prevent further rages:

1. Talk together about strategies for when the rumbling anger is felt. Discuss their rumbling 'symptoms'. What can they do to prevent an explosion in future?

2. What was it that triggered the rage? Use the cartooning exercise on page 97 to help the student identify triggers and work out what to do next time a trigger occurs.

3. Maybe a small thing in the classroom was enough to spark the rage – a cold draught ruffling their hair, a scratchy bit on the chair, too much noise. Help your student to identify their ideal learning environment so you can pre-empt further rages.

Closing the cycle

Ideally, your student should be engaged in some absorbing task when the rest of the class returns. Remember, all that's happened is they have expressed pent-up anger and frustration. If you present it as no big deal, it is less likely to be seen as one by the rest of the class. Of course, much of their reaction will depend on how inclusive your school is and how much they know about Asperger syndrome. They will probably still want to talk with you about it.

It's a good idea to talk to the other pupils in your class about anger. They will have their own ideas and examples to share, and the discussion may help them to understand better what has happened.

Policy and procedures

It is important to remember that rage is not part of every Asperger student's behaviour but you and your school do need to have a policy and procedures in place for rage attacks. These are the key considerations:

1. Where will you send the other pupils and how will you get them to leave the room?
2. Do you need to send another member of staff with them? If so, who?
3. How will you get help and who will come? Will that person have the authority to make important decisions?
4. How long will that person take to reach you? Rages are usually over very quickly.
5. Although straightforward classrooms are not too difficult to keep safe, what about a science lab, a technology room, the library, the canteen?
6. Where can your student sleep, if necessary?
7. What will you tell the rest of the class about what has happened?
8. What are you going to tell parents? Pupils take home all sorts of stories that can perpetrate myths and distort the real picture.

Summary

- Inappropriate behaviour and rage is almost always a reaction to extreme stress
- Rage is nothing more than suppressed extreme anger and frustration
- There are three stages to the cycle – rage can only be averted during the first stage
- There are a number of strategies to try to prevent full-blown rage
- If the student proceeds to 'meltdown', it has to run its course
- Focus on the safety of other students, the raging student and yourself
- After the rage, stay with the student during the recovery period
- This valuable time can be used for discussing what has happened and how to prevent future incidents
- The school must have a clear and coherent policy and drill for student rage

What is Asperger Syndrome?

 Social Interaction

 Obsessive Interests

 Repetition & Change

 Verbal & Non-verbal Communication

 Whirling Mind & Unusual Sensitivities

 Anger & Rage

 Inclusion ◀

Inclusion

Being inclusive

This final section looks at a range of whole-school challenges in relation to Asperger syndrome pupils. It clarifies what we mean by inclusion, looks at how to support Asperger students in **study skills, problem solving** and **exams,** examines the roles of **pastoral and support staff** and considers strategies for **outside the classroom**.

Inclusion does **not** mean placing students with disabilities or learning differences into a mainstream class and allowing them to stay there provided they learn to 'fit in' with the rest of the class.

It does **not** mean giving them a learning support assistant who is expected to adapt the status quo of the classroom just for 'their student'.

Inclusion means **all school staff** adapting the environment, classroom, teaching, learning and school to the needs of the students within it. The school has to make sufficient adjustment to itself and the curriculum to accommodate all its young people.

Implications for all staff

Every member of staff in school should know the Asperger pupils' needs, triggers and characteristics. In addition all staff should:

- Be aware of bullying and teasing, to which Asperger pupils are particularly vulnerable
- Understand that Asperger pupils may not conform to school or social norms and rules because they do not know them. If a member of staff criticises or, worse, punishes these students for doing the wrong thing, it's possible they are, in reality, being punished for having the syndrome
- Be aware that pupils with the syndrome will be distressed by inconsistency and by not knowing what is happening next. It is essential to be consistent
- Know what contingencies are in place for possible incidents during breaks, lunchtimes and lessons outside the classroom

Implications for pastoral staff

If you have overall responsibility for the wellbeing of an Asperger pupil in your school:

- Ensure all staff are thoroughly trained in the implications of having an Asperger student in the school (This includes senior managers, new teachers at their induction, governors and any other policy-makers.)

- Ensure as much consistency throughout the school and the staff as possible. (This is not a desirable *element* of success for the student – it is *essential*.)

- Make sure the student has a named person to whom they can go whenever there is a problem – and that there is a deputy for when that person is away

- Work closely with the parents. Some parents are reluctant to admit their child has special needs – occasionally the parent has the syndrome too. You need to be diplomatic but still talk about the strategies you are using in school with this student and the need for close communication at all times. Remember, there is nothing 'wrong' with their child – he or she is, like all of us, different

Implications for pastoral staff

- Meet at least weekly with the student. The time and day should be set in stone and if you are absent, your 'deputy' should be there. Use the time to discuss school or problems, or just relax. The more informal this meeting, the better

- Explain rules and expectations to the student and set clear boundaries and parameters for behaviour. (This works best in organisations where rules and boundaries already exist and where there is consistency across the staff)

- Remember that the school needs to fit in with the student rather than the other way round, so you need to know the pupil very well to be able to convey information and strategies to other staff

- Avoid battles of wills with the student – you'll never win. Instead, give choices, each accompanied by a consequence. So, rather than telling the student they will stay in at break for not working, say: *'You can carry on messing about, in which case you will stay in to finish your work at break, or you can finish the work now and you can go to break first. I don't mind – it is up to you.'* This appeals to Asperger logic and will save either one of you losing face

The role of the LSA

Because of the need for consistency, it is ideal if the pupil can work with the same learning support assistant, or no more than two, during their time in school. If this is impossible, all LSAs working with the pupil need to work in exactly the same way, fitting in with the student's needs.

If you are the LSA, you'll find you're often not needed for academic support. Many students with the syndrome are very able and feel frustrated at not being allowed to get on with the one thing they excel at in school – academic work. There are, however, plenty of other areas where your input is invaluable. These can be negotiated between the school, the student and you, the LSA. I've made suggestions below:

- **Interpreter** Some staff may communicate in a way that is incomprehensible to your students, relying heavily on metaphor, pauses and non-verbal communication, for instance. You can be helpful in interpreting this foreign language for the Asperger student and in explaining the communication complications to the teacher

The role of the LSA

- **Organiser** Can you be the person with the checklists, the colour-coding, the labelled and indexed files, the timetables etc? Can you be the timekeeper, the holder of the stationery, the keeper of the appointment diary? Yes, we want the *pupil* to accept responsibility for these things, especially as they get older, but who is going to train them?

- **Social skills trainer** I know of several LSAs who run social skills training sessions for students during the lunch break or after school. Not only is this a chance to enhance your own skills and expertise, but you will also be working with your student(s) on possibly the most important things they need to know

- **Parent coordinator** If you are the main communicator with parents it will enhance your relationship with the student as well as raising your profile in the school. You may find your role with your Asperger student is more like that of a parent – you become a guide, a help and advisor, and a mentor

The role of the LSA

Advocate

As you will probably know your student better than anyone else in the school, you can advocate for them with others. Even better if you can teach them to advocate for themselves:

'I have Asperger syndrome. It does not stop me doing a........., b......... and c........., but I do have some problems with x........, y........ and z......... and for them I have the following strategies...................'

Friend

This is probably your most important role – a 'mate', a confidante, someone who is always there in times of trouble or bewilderment. You're the person who can stop the planet wobbling

There is also a key role for LSAs and other staff to play in helping pupils with study skills and problem-solving, and with smoothing their path in examinations.

Study skills and organisation

Many people with Asperger syndrome also have dyslexia and/or dyspraxia and the associated lack of organisational skills. Berating the pupil for forgetting equipment or bringing the wrong books to school will only distress them further. It's far better to put some organisational strategies in place.

For every classroom activity and homework, your student should be able to answer: What am I doing? Why am I doing it? How should I be doing it? How will I know when I am finished? What should I do next?

A set of **printed organising sheets** kept by teachers or the LSA can help – and check verbally with the student that they know the answers to the above questions.

Homework books, in which pupils write themselves, are of limited use. More valuable is **a notebook** that is carried between school and home via which parents and teachers can communicate. Parents can alert staff to how their child is feeling and how they coped with homework, etc; teachers can alert parents to how that child is learning and any specific strategies they are using.

Study skills and organisation

Students with the syndrome tend to be visual learners, so they like things to look at:

- **Handouts** should always be available to reinforce the lesson, preferably with important points already highlighted
- Concepts and ideas will be better understood if they are accompanied by **charts, diagrams** or **pictures**
- Organising tools such as **checklists and colour codes** are immensely useful, provided they are used consistently throughout the school
- Students will feel more secure with **lesson agendas** and **rigid routines**
- **Rubrics** to accompany homework will help students to improve their own work

Many Asperger students find it difficult to ask for help. Always check with the student that they have understood.

Support for problem solving

Problem solving is often difficult for Asperger pupils, not because of low brain capacity, but because they are lateral thinkers. They may give a totally logical answer but not what the teacher expected (nor what the examiner wanted).

If setting problems, be very clear about what you want. In maths, for example, if you set a problem to test your student's grasp of a concept, be clear about that in the question and tell your student what the answer should look like.

The sort of problem that has to be solved by a group of pupils working with a simulated situation may be very difficult for Asperger students, as the simulation itself may be seen as illogical.

Ironically, the kind of problem-solving skills Asperger students have tend to be valued in the workplace as 'out of the box thinking'. This is not always what is wanted in school tasks or exams.

Other difficulties with problem solving

Multiple choice questions are difficult for many students, but especially for those with Asperger syndrome, who can often find perfectly logical reasons for all the answers being valid.

It is a useful exercise for all students to learn how to answer these questions but if it's possible to choose a syllabus that doesn't include multiple choice, that would take away one more pressure from a student with the syndrome.

Because of their lack of social imagination, people with Asperger syndrome also find **abstract concepts** difficult. Where possible, illustrate the concept with examples from real life or from the pupil's interest area.

Examination strategies

Exams are stressful for everyone and even more stressful to Asperger students if they do not know what to expect. A few strategies put in place in advance will pave the way for as stress-free an experience as possible:

- As soon as possible, inform your student exactly what is going to happen, where, and when. Help them to work out their own timetables – including revision timetables, and a structured revision guide
- Let the student know as soon as you can which room they will be in, which seat, and who the invigilator will be. If they are to be in a large exam hall, which other students will be there?

It may be possible to provide a separate exam room for your student (in which case any self-soothing behaviours used to keep calm, such as tapping a pencil or humming, can be accommodated) and an invigilator they know and trust. If the latter can be arranged, the invigilator must be briefed about triggers, anxieties and signs of stress in order to pre-empt incidents.

Breaks and lunchtimes

Breaks and lunchtimes are not always pleasurable times for Asperger pupils.

Anna preferred to take a book onto the field and sit quietly to read it. Her teacher told her she should go and play with the others instead.

Luke liked to go off on his own and have imaginary fights with the aliens in his favourite cartoons. The other students laughed at him and called him names.

Robert, aged seven, was so frightened at the thought of going into a noisy, chaotic playground that he panicked, lashed out and broke his teacher's jaw. Following instant exclusion, no other school would take him because he had been labelled 'violent'.

If breaks are meant to refresh and relax, why put your pupils into a stressful environment? Are there places they can go instead of the playground?

Outside the classroom

It's not just breaks and lunchtimes when 'incidents' are more likely to happen.
In the classroom there is structure, routine, and clear relationships are in place.
Outside the classroom these things are often absent. Provision needs to be made for:

* The canteen at lunchtime

* The library – often a place Asperger pupils visit at lunch or break

* PE and sports lessons (although your students may be athletic, do they know the rules of the games they are trying to play?)

* Home time

* Travelling to and from school

* Breaks between classes – especially corridor etiquette

* Out of school visits

None of these need pose any problems, provided everybody knows of possible issues and contingencies are in place.

Common sense – don't make assumptions

Although you are possibly dealing with a student with very high academic ability, the apparent absence of common sense may surprise you. **Don't assume that what is obvious to you is obvious to your Asperger pupil**.

Amy had been told on numerous occasions by her mother not to take a hairdryer into the bath. She did not realise this also applied to the shower.

Omar sat in the same place on the reading mat every day. On Thursday, most of the class were elsewhere, rehearsing for the school play, but Omar refused to move from his usual place even though there was nobody now in front of him.

Leroy was told to write 400 words on the Spanish Inquisition. He stopped after exactly 400 words, even though he was in the middle of a sentence.

A sign on **James's** bus said 'Please have correct change ready'. He assumed that without the correct change he'd not be allowed on the bus. On those days he walked to school and was late!

What about the other students?

A common dilemma faced by schools is what to tell the other pupils about their Asperger classmates. Is it better to identify and label Asperger pupils or to avoid 'stigmatising' them by saying nothing?

Personally, I think it depends on the way your organisation looks at diversity and disability. How much do the staff and students at your school know about learning diversity? Are we talking 'disability' or 'different ability'? If you have a 'syndrome' does it automatically mean there is something 'wrong' with you?

Schools have made great progress in racial and religious harmony by teaching about race and religion. Why not discuss learning differences and abilities too? You don't have to name anyone – pupils usually know who you are talking about. Even better, get the pupils themselves to discuss their differences, perhaps emphasising that for every problem a condition presents, it provides a strength by way of compensation.

The more staff and pupils accept that we are all different, with our own strengths and weaknesses, the more we can celebrate the quirks and the joys of being ourselves.

Summary

- It is important for all school staff to work round the student, not vice versa
- All staff should know the implications of having that student in that school at that time
- Study skills and organisation strategies may be particularly difficult and need constant reinforcement
- People with Asperger syndrome solve problems differently from how we may expect
- If you put strategies for exams in place early, that will ease exam stress
- Pastoral staff play a very important role
- The LSA's role may not be the same as it is when working with other students
- Strategies for outside the classroom are as important as strategies within it
- Although your student may be clever, it doesn't mean they have 'common sense'
- Rather than telling the other pupils just about your Asperger student, celebrate the diversity among all of us

Further reading and resources

General background reading

Asperger Syndrome: A Guide for Parents and Professionals by Tony Attwood. Published by Jessica Kingsley, 1997

Freaks, Geeks and Asperger Syndrome: A User Guide to Adolescence by Luke Jackson. Published by Jessica Kingsley, 2002

Martian in the Playground: Understanding the Schoolchild with Asperger's Syndrome by Claire Sainsbury. Published by Lucky Duck Publishing Ltd, 2000

Working with younger children

Guidelines for Working with Children with ASD at Foundation Stage and Key Stage 1 by South Gloucestershire Council. Published by The National Autistic Society, 2005

Inclusion in the Primary Classroom: Support Materials for Children with Autistic Spectrum Disorders by Joy Beaney and Penny Kershaw. Published by The National Autistic Society, 2003

Play With Me: Including Children with Autism in Mainstream Primary Schools by Isabel Cottinelli Telmo. Published by The National Autistic Society, 2004

Further reading and resources

Behaviour management

Asperger Syndrome and Difficult Moments: Practical Solutions for Tantrums, Rage and Meltdowns by Brenda Smith Myles and Jack Southwick. Published by Autism Asperger Publishing, 2005

Conflict in the Classroom by N.J. Long, W.C. Morse and R.G. Newman, Belmont CA, 1976

The Incredible 5-point scale by Kari Dunn Buron and Mitzi Curtis. Published by Autism Asperger Publishing Co, 2003

A Teacher's Guide to Co-operative Discipline. How to Manage Your Classroom and Promote Self-esteem. Published by Circle Pines MN American Guidance Service, 1989

Understanding and Managing the Acting Out Child by M. Beck. Published by The Pointer, 1985

To help communication skills

Interactive Music Therapy – A Positive Approach. Therapy at a Child Development Centre by Amelia Oldfield. Published by Jessica Kingsley, 2006

Interactive Music Therapy in Child and Family Psychiatry: Clinical Practice, Research and Teaching by Amelia Oldfield. Published by Jessica Kingsley, 2006

What Did You Say? What Do You Mean? An Illustrated Guide to Understanding Metaphors by Jude Walton and Jane Telford. Published by Jessica Kingsley, 2004

Further reading and resources

To assist social skills training

Body Language and Communication: A Guide for People with Autistic Spectrum Disorders by S Perks. Published by The National Autistic Society, 2007

Developing Social Interaction and Understanding: A Resource for Working with Children and Young People with Autistic Spectrum Disorders by Fiona Knott and Aline-Wendy Dunlop. Published by The National Autistic Society, 2007

My Social Stories Book by Carol Gray. Published by Jessica Kingsley, 2001

Revealing the Hidden Social Code: Social Stories for People with Autistic Spectrum Disorder by Carol Gray et al. Published by Jessica Kingsley, 2005

Young Friends by S. Roffey, T. Tarrant and K. Majors. Published by Cassell, 1994

Software and accessories

Mind Reading: The Interactive Guide to Emotions by Cambridge University Autism Research Centre. Published by Jessica Kingsley, 2005

ISPEEK at Home and *ISPEEK at School* by Janet Dixon. Published by Jessica Kingsley, 2007

Inspiration software for visual mapping of ideas at **www.techready.co.uk**

Time Timer (for time management) The National Autistic Society

Social Skills Stickers (rewards stickers) The National Autistic Society

Websites and acknowledgements

www.nas.org.uk (The National Autistic Society)

www.oasis.co.uk

www.neron-learning.co.uk (for help with social skills and communications)

www.autism.org.uk/asperger

www.aspergerfoundation.org.uk

Acknowledgements

I would like to thank the various teachers and learning support assistants who supplied me with many of the anecdotes and examples in this book, and Luke and Ashley for their Asperger point of view. Thanks, Jan, for the endless proof-reading and for keeping me going when I showed signs of flagging. Thank you, Linda, for being such a calm and patient midwife at the birth of this, my first book. Finally, thank you, Jonathan, for helping me to understand motherhood, for making me a more compassionate and knowledgeable education professional, and for teaching me far more about life and people than I could ever teach you.

About the author

Ronnie Young

Ronnie Young has been a teacher all her working life, in settings as diverse as schools, pupil referral units, offender institutions and further education. She is now a consultant and trainer specialising in behaviour management and neuro-diversity, most notably autistic spectrum disorder. She is a practising Ofsted inspector in both mainstream and specialist education.

Her son was not identified as having Asperger syndrome until he was 18, so Ronnie understands at first hand the difficulties people with the condition experience in school. She knows the difference a proper diagnosis and appropriate support can make. Ronnie works for The National Autistic Society as a trainer and consultant and is a regular contributor to national conferences. She spends much of her time training and supporting staff in schools and colleges here and in the US. She is happy to be contacted by any organisation seeking tailor-made training: ronnie.young@blueyonder.co.uk

Order Form

Your details

Name _____

Position _____

School _____

Address _____

_____

_____

Telephone _____

Fax _____

E-mail _____

VAT No. (EC only) _____

Your Order Ref _____

Please send me:

No. copies

Asperger Syndrome _____ Pocketbook [ ]

_____ Pocketbook [ ]

_____ Pocketbook [ ]

_____ Pocketbook [ ]

Order by Post

Teachers' Pocketbooks
Laurel House, Station Approach
Alresford, Hants. SO24 9JH UK

Order by Phone, Fax or Internet
Telephone: +44 (0)1962 735573
Facsimile: +44 (0)1962 733637
E-mail: sales@teacherspocketbooks.co.uk
Web: www.teacherspocketbooks.co.uk

Customers in USA should contact:
2427 Bond Street, University Park, IL 60466
Tel: 866 620 6944   Facsimile: 708 534 7803
E-mail: mp.orders@ware-pak.com
Web: www.managementpocketbooks.com